Explorations in Corpus Linguistics

Michael McCarthy

CAMBRIDGE
UNIVERSITY PRESS

CAMBRIDGE UNIVERSITY PRESS
Cambridge, New York, Melbourne, Madrid, Cape Town, Singapore, São Paulo

Cambridge University Press
32 Avenue of the Americas, New York, NY 10013-2473, USA

www.cambridge.org

© Cambridge University Press 2006

First published 2006

Printed in the United States of America

ISBN-13 978-0-521-   paperback

Book layout services: Page Designs International

Reprinted with Permission:
"Fluency and confluence," *The Language Teacher*, vol. 21, 2002. Japan Association for Language Teaching, pp. 30-52.
"This that and the other," *Teanga: The Irish Yearbook of Applied Linguistics*, vol. 21, 2002 [2004], pp. 30-52.
"Ten criteria for a spoken grammar," *New Perspectives on Grammar Teaching in Second Language*, LEA, Inc. pp. 51-75.

Table of Contents

1 Fluency and confluence: What fluent speakers do   **1**

2 *This that and the other*: Multi-word clusters in spoken English as visible patterns of interaction   7

3 Ten criteria for a spoken grammar   **27**

1

Fluency and confluence: What fluent speakers do

Reprinted with Permission: *The Language Teacher*, vol. 29, November 6, 2005. Japan Association for Language Teaching, pp. 26–28.

Michael McCarthy
University of Nottingham, University of Limerick, and the Pennsylvania State University

Abstract

In "Fluency and Confluence," Michael McCarthy examines the notion of fluency and reviews factors that are often assumed to contribute to it: rate of talk, lack of pauses, natural rhythm and stress. Contrasting these idealized criteria with observed native-speaker conversations calls into question the validity of long-held assumptions. The author points toward a modified definition of fluency that de-emphasizes monologic performance in favor of the skillful use of chunks (high-frequency multi-word phrases) and the cooperative construction of meaning across speaker turns in dialogue.

Introduction

In many respects the nature of fluency in spoken language is under-researched, despite the fact that the term is deeply embedded in lay linguistic perceptions as well as in professional considerations. For instance, the words "I am fluent in [language x]" will return tens of thousands of hits on Google and the term *fluency* is used widely in the applied linguistics and language teaching literature. Lennon (1990) underlines the less than sharp delineation of the concept in noting that the term *fluency* is often used as a cover-all for general oral proficiency, as well as to refer to a more restricted component of proficiency (e.g., in the way it often appears as one of a list of factors for assessment of proficiency in oral examinations). Most dominant in the literature over a long period, however, has been the debate on *fluency* versus *accuracy* (Brumfit, 1984; Hammerly, 1991; Richards, Platt, & Webber, 1985). Fluency (viewed as unfettered, meaning-focused performance) is often assumed to be something different from accuracy (viewed more as reflective, form-focused performance), though Brumfit (1984) notes that fluent language does not necessarily imply inaccurate language. Furthermore, both are studied as variables in investigations into the output of task-based learning, where conditions such as the presence or absence of pre-planning are seen to affect fluency, or accuracy, or both (Ellis 2003; Foster & Skehan, 1999).

Fillmore (1979) famously characterized fluency as including the ability to talk at length without abnormal pauses, the ability to talk coherently, employing *semantically dense* sentences, the ability to have appropriate things to say in a broad range of contexts, and the ability to be imaginative and creative in language use. Later, Brumfit (1984) argued that fluency involved *natural* use of language and that continuity and speed were involved. Schmidt (1992) also includes an element of *automaticity,* or the ability to retrieve language forms immediately and without conscious searching, in the characterization of fluency. In dictionary entries too, we find an emphasis on rate of speaking and automaticity. Hartmann and Stork's (1976) definition of fluency includes the notion of automaticity and *normal conversational speed* (p. 86). Automaticity presumably brings with it the accuracy of form which the fluent native speaker seems to display effortlessly. Another dictionary entry, by Richards, Platt, and Weber (1985), includes mention of native-like rhythm, intonation, stress, and rate of speaking. This aligns with the frequent attention paid to prosodic factors in fluency, so-called *phonological fluency* (Pennington, 1989). Some linguists additionally point to other factors that must be held in consideration in adjudging fluency, such as distinguishing knowledge *about* language and the procedural ability to *use* it appropriately (Fillmore, 1979; Schmidt, 1992).

The question I wish to explore here is whether an emphasis on rate of talk, lack of pausing, the presence of particular phonological qualities such as natural rhythm and stress are the whole of (or even the most important part of) the story. If we look at native speaker corpora of natural language use, we find ourselves in the presence of large numbers of what would typically be judged as fluent speakers, who perform accurately in the sense that none of the lexico-grammatical principles—such as normative grammar and appropriate collocation—are violated. But we will not always find those speakers performing at speed, not pausing, using ideal rhythm, and so on. In fact their performance often appears dysfluent by some of the criteria mentioned above. In the following extract from the North American spoken component of the Cambridge International Corpus, the speakers are talking about what to do and where to go in Italy. The conversation does not seem to present any problems of comprehension to the interlocutors, and, as already stated is *accurate*, yet it seems in parts, by any standards, disjointed:

> A: Where would you tell me to go? And then to a two week trip. Where would you tell me to go?
> B: Okay. Um well let's see. You're gonna want to . . . You're gonna want to see I mean since you're there for two weeks you're you're probably gonna you know you're just gonna have to see the . . . You're not gonna have time to really wander around and so you're gonna want to go where the churches are and+
> A: Uh-huh.
> B: +the museums are+
> A: Uh-huh.
> B: +so I would say go to Rome and go to Florence and point . . . I mean I could you know I could probably tell you small small little churches that aren't you know the huge uh Saint Peters+
> A: Right.
> B: +like this but . . .
> A: But in made the honor in the guide books or whatever.
> B: Right.
> A: Uh-huh.
> B: Right. Right. Um you know but so I'd say definitely hit the big cities and I don't know some people are no and my friends parents went over there and they asked me the same question and they were renting a car just and that really allows you a lot of freedom because especially in I mean all over Italy really there are just these tiny you know tiny towns that ha= you know that are easily accessible by car+
> A: Uh-huh.
> B: +with like monasteries and woods. It's big and that you just sort of have to pull off and be like 'Oh I don't know what this is all about but let's [laughing] just+
> A: Let's check it out.

B: +park and go see'.

What then, makes these speakers fluent, or should we condemn them as dysfluent and as bad examples, especially for language pedagogy? In some senses they do live up to the classic criteria for fluency: they talk continuously, appropriately, without awkward pauses. Where speaker B does pause (indicated by . . .) it is usually in order to re-cast the utterance, something native-speakers and non-native speakers need to do constantly, though in the non-native this is often deemed to be evidence of a problem or of poor proficiency. On the other hand, sentences are left half-finished, and there are numerous apparent redundancies and hesitations.

I would like, nonetheless, to suggest that three significant aspects of the conversational extract make it a model of fluency rather than dysfluency.

1. The speakers do fulfill some of the central criteria established in the literature, as discussed above.

2. Both speakers use formulaic chunks, one of the key elements contributing to speech rate and conversational flow, but only recently beginning to be fully researched in corpora of spoken language use.

3. The conversation itself is fluent. Speakers contribute to each others' fluency; they scaffold each other's performance and make the whole conversation flow. There is a confluence in the talk, like two rivers flowing inseperable together.

In relation to (2) the conversation contains high-frequency chunks which occur in the top 1000 list for that length of chunk in the spoken segment of the Cabridge Inernational Corpus (the rank is in parenthesis, based on the 2-word chunk frequency list, the 3-word list, etc.):

And then (14)
I mean (12)
You know (1)
You're gonna (665)
I would say (227)
Or whatever (502)
I don't know (2)

There are also chunks of lower frequency—*let's see, let's check it out,* etc. Chunks, by their nature, are retrieved whole; they are not created anew each time; they are part of that automaticity which enables effortless accuracy. They operate either as sentence frames to which new content may be attached (e.g., *you're gonna* . . .) or as pragmatically specialized units, i.e., self-contained units which have developed specific pragmatic functions (e.g., *or whatever,* used to refer vaguely to shared categories). They are typically spoken quickly and as one tone unit; they are thus part of phonological fluency as well as lexico-grammatical fluency. The rest of the utterance (i.e., the newly synthesized, non-chunked content elements) can be spoken more slowly without damaging fluency. The reverse (slow chunks and fast content) is more difficult to contemplate as sounding fluent. Speed is not everything, at least not constantly rapid talk; some parts of conversations may be uttered rapidly, but it may often be desirable to slow down in crucial parts of one's message.

In relation to characteristic (3), a socioculturally embedded notion of conversation sees speakers as supporting one another, in other words as "scaffolding" each other's performance, in Vygotsky's terms (Vygotsky, 1978), either by back-channelling (*uh-huh, right*) or by predicting and completing each other's turns (B: . . . *but let's* [laughing] *just+* A: *Let's check it out.*). The conversation, and its flow, are seen as a *joint* responsibility, and our perception of fluency, I would argue, is much influenced by the cooperatively created flow of talk, rather than just the talent of one individual speaker.

In sum, the notion of fluency has its roots in linguistic qualities related to lexico-grammatical and phonological flow accompanied by apparently effortless accurate selection of elements, created by individual speakers, and in the ability of participants to converse appropriately on topics, but also, crucially, in the ability to retrieve chunks, and in the degree of interactive support each speaker gives to the flow of talk, helping one another to be fluent and creating a confluence in the conversation. Judging a speaker on monologic performance, on an oral examination where assessors hold back from interacting like normal conversational partners, or basing measures of fluency on solo performances of read speech analyzed by speech recognition software which counts speech rates, pauses, and so forth (Cucchiarini, Strik, & Boves, 2000), would seem to be missing a great deal of what fluency really is.

References

Brumfit, C. (1984). *Communicative methodology in language teaching: The roles of fluency and accuracy.* Cambridge: Cambridge University Press.

Cucchiarini, C., Strik, H., & Boves, L. (2000). Quantitative assessment of second language learners' fluency by means of automatic speech recognition technology. *Journal of the Acoustical Society of America,* 107(2), 989-999.

Ellis, R. (2003). *Task-based Language Learning and Teaching.* Oxford: Oxford University Press.

Fillmore, C. J. (1979). On fluency. In C. J. Fillmore, D. Kempler, & W. S. Y. Wang (Eds.), *Individual differences in language ability and language behaviour* (pp. 85-102). New York: Academic Press.

Foster, P. & Skehan, P. (1999). The influence of source of planning and focus of planning on task-based performance. *Language Teaching Research,* 3(3), 215-247.

Hammerly, H. (1991). *Fluency and accuracy: Toward balance in language teaching and learning.* Clevedon, UK: Multilingual Matters.

Hartmann, R. R. K., & Stork, F. C. (1976). *Dictionary of language and linguistics.* New York: Wiley.

Lennon, P. (1990). Investigating fluency in EFL: A qualitative approach. *Language Learning,* 40(3), 387-417.

Pennington, M. C. (1989). Teaching pronunciation from the top down. *RELC Journal,* 20(1): 20-38.

Richards, J. C., Platt, J., & Weber, H. (1985). *Longman dictionary of applied linguistics.* London: Longman.

Schmidt, R. (1992). Psychological mechanisms underlying language fluency. *Studies in Second Language Acquisition,* 14, 357-385.

Vygotsky L (1978) *Mind in Society: The Development of Higher Psychological Processes.* Cambridge, Mass: Harvard University Press.

2 This that and the other: *Multi-word clusters in spoken English as visible patterns of interaction*

Reprinted with Permission: *Teanga: The Irish Yearbook of Applied Linguistics*, vol. 21, 2002 [2004], pp. 30-52.

Michael McCarthy
University of Nottingham, UK/ University of Limerick

Ronald Carter
University of Nottingham, UK

Abstract

This paper investigates multi-word strings automatically retrieved from a 5-million word corpus of conversational English from Britain and Ireland. Many such strings have neither syntactic nor semantic integrity, for example *at the, it was a, what do you*. However, many strings display pragmatic integrity, encoding interactive functions such as hedging, vagueness, discourse marking, etc. Examples include *and that sort of thing, you know, a couple of*. We identify the most common pragmatically integrated clusters and discuss their functions, and compare their frequency with single words, illustrating that many clusters are more frequent than single words accepted as belonging to the core vocabulary of English. The clusters also contrast with the low frequency of opaque idiomatic expressions. High-frequency clusters raise issues around the distinction between lexis and grammar, and support a synthetic view of language production and storage, with implications for the understanding of notions such as fluency and idiomaticity.

Introduction

The single word

In the study of the lexicon, the single word has remained, until recently, relatively unchallenged as the basic unit of meaning and as the focus in the study of lexical acquisition in second and foreign languages. This is not without good reason: single words form a substantial part of the lexicon of English and are perceived in pedagogy as the central units to be acquired. Other units consisting of more than one word, such as phrasal verbs, compounds, and idioms, are often thought of as items belonging to higher levels of achievement. There are, of course, exceptions to this: greetings and other phatic expressions (e.g., *How's it going?, See you soon, Thanks a lot*), specialized functional phrases (e.g., *Happy birthday, Good luck*), basic prepositional phrases (e.g., *in the morning, at home*), and common compounds (e.g., *car park, check-in*) are often taught and/or acquired even at elementary level.

Collocation

Recent developments in the study of lexis have generated new applications within lexicography and language teaching, offering the possibility of a better understanding of the nature of the lexicon, especially multi-word phenomena. The most important of these developments can be seen in the Neo-Firthian approach to word meaning. Firth (1935) famously proposed that the meaning of a word was as much a matter of how the word combined in context with other words (i.e., its collocations) as any inherent properties of meaning it possessed of itself: *dark* is part of the meaning of *night*, and vice-versa, through their high probability of co-occurrence in texts (Firth 1951/1957). Collocations are not absolute or 100 percent deterministic, but are the probabilistic outcomes of repeated combinations created and experienced by language users. We talk of being *madly in love* in preference to (but not in absolute exclusion or prohibition of) being *crazily in love*; tea is usually *strong*, but cars are *powerful;* and so on. Key discussions of the implications of Firth's theory of collocation appear in Halliday (1966) and Sinclair (1966). Both Halliday and Sinclair foresaw in those papers the development of the computational analysis of lexis using large amounts of text. Collocation studies show, most importantly, that a good deal of semantically transparent vocabulary is to a greater or lesser degree fossilized into restricted patterns (see also Aisenstadt 1981). The notion of collocation shifts the emphasis from the single word to pairs of words as integrated chunks of meaning, and collocation has become an uncontroversial element in a good deal of language description and pedagogy.

Words in corpora

The growth of corpus linguistics (see McCarthy 1998: Chapter 1 for a brief historical sketch) has convinced linguists that vocabulary is much more than the 'unordered list of all lexical formatives' which Chomsky (1965:84) referred to it as. Pioneering studies of large corpora by linguists such as Sinclair (1991) have shown lexis to be a far more powerful influence in the basic organization of language and of meaning than was ever previously conceived. Corpora reveal the regular, patterned preferences for modes of expression of language users in given contexts, and show how large numbers of users separated in time and space repeatedly orient towards the same language patterns when involved in comparable social activities. Corpora reveal that much of our lexical output consists of multi-word units; language occurs in ready-made chunks to a far greater extent than could ever be accommodated by a theory of language insistent upon the primacy of syntax.

Sinclair (1987, 1991), based on his lexicographic studies of collocation in the Birmingham Collection of English Text (later known as The Bank of English), sees two fundamental principles at work in the creation of meaning. These he calls the *idiom principle* and the *open choice principle*. The *idiom principle* is the central one in the creation of text and meaning in speech and writing, and works on the basis of the speaker/writer having at his/her disposal a large store of ready-made lexico-grammatical chunks. Syntax, far from being primary, is only brought into service occasionally, as a kind of 'glue' to cement the chunks together.

Sinclair (1996) sees form and meaning as complementary: different senses of a word will characteristically be realized in different structural configurations. This extends the original notion of collocation to encompass longer strings of words and includes their preferred grammatical configurations or *colligations* (see also Mitchell 1971). The unitary consequences of collocation and colligation produce meaningful strings or chunks which are stored in memory (see also Bolinger 1976) and which substantiate the idiom principle.

Corpus-based work on grammar has had similar consequences, especially in the research of Biber and his associates (Biber et al. 1999). Biber et al. examine a wide range of recurrent expressions, even though many of them are not 'idiomatic' in the sense of being semantically opaque, and even though they may be syntactically incomplete (see the discussion below), and they term such strings *lexical bundles* (see also Biber and Conrad 1999). Significant recurrence is defined by establishing frequency cut-off points, for example, that a string must occur at least 10 times per million words of text (or 20 times in the case of Cortes 2002), and must be distributed over a number of different texts. This means that a bundle might consist of a syntactically incomplete but meaningful string such as *to be able to* or *a lot of the,* examples offered by Cortes (2002), along with more obviously semantically- and pragmatically-integrated expressions such as *as a result of* and *on the other hand*. Those investigating lexical bundles generally argue that the bundles operate as important structuring devices in texts and are register- (or genre-) sensitive. Oakey (2002) demonstrates that common recurring strings such as *it has been [shown/observed/argued/etc] that,* which are used to introduce external evidence in writing, are differently distributed across three genres. Furthermore, the presence (or absence) of lexical bundles in second-language learner output has been considered a useful measure of comparison and evaluation of learner competence vis-à-vis native speaker competence (see De Cock 1998, 2000; see also Granger 1998).

Phraseology and idiomaticity

Developments arising from corpus-based studies have been paralleled, over the years, by non-corpus-based research into multi-word lexical units. The general field of phraseology and the study of idiomaticity have contributed to our understanding of multi-word phenomena, both in the West and (at the same time but often unknown to Western linguists) in the former Soviet Union (see Kunin 1970; Benson and Benson 1993). Such linguists have long worked within frameworks not dominated by syntax.

In the literature, discussion usually centres upon the semantics, the syntax, the cross-linguistic differences and the universality of opaque idiomatic expressions (Makkai 1978; Fernando and Flavell 1981), which, by and large, are relatively rare in occurrence in everyday conversation. But there has also been useful and illuminating research into everyday conversational routines, gambits, and discourse markers which has involved a recognition of the multi-word nature of such items (see Coulmas 1979, 1981a, and b). However, few idiomatologists have gone so far as to examine idiom use in naturally-occurring spoken data, an exception being Strässler (1982), and more recently Powell (1992).

McCarthy (1998) lists different formal and functional types of idiomatic expression which were found through manually searching the CANCODE spoken corpus, the corpus on which the present paper is based (see below). McCarthy's purpose in that categorization was to show that a wide range of idiomatic fixed expressions occur in everyday conversation, both formally and functionally, perhaps wider than that suggested by the traditional emphasis on *verb + object* idioms (e.g., *kick the bucket, pass the buck*) in language pedagogy.

The study of multi-word units has also focused on how they have developed pragmatic specialisms in regular contexts of use (e.g., Bolinger 1976; Cowie 1988; Nattinger and deCarrico 1992; Lewis 1993; and Howarth 1998). Multi-word expressions have additionally come under the scrutiny of sociolinguists and conversation analysts, where the purpose is to judge the social significance of the moment of placement and use of particular items. Drew and Holt (1998), for instance, show that idiomatic expressions occur regularly at places of topic-transition and as summaries of gist. Such work underlines the non-random use of idiomatic expressions and strengthens the claims of the present paper that investigating multi-word phenomena can tell us much about the nature of interaction.

Different terminology has been used to describe the phenomena of interest to us here, including *lexical phrases* (Nattinger and deCarrico 1992), *prefabricated patterns* (Hakuta 1974), *routine formulae* (Coulmas 1979), *formulaic sequences* (Wray 2000, 2002), *lexicalized stems* (Pawley and Syder 1983), *chunks* (De Cock 2000), as well as the more conventionally-understood labels such as *(restricted) collocations, fixed expressions, multi-word units/expressions, idioms,* etc. Whatever the terminology, multi-word phenomena seem to be central to a wide range of linguistic and applied linguistic preoccupations. 'Off-the-peg' vocabulary enables fluent production in real time, and would seem to be at least as significant as the single-word elements that compose texts when it comes to investigating either the semantics or the pragmatics of language. Indeed, one can hardly imagine language not being (at least in part) produced ready-assembled (see Bolinger 1976).

In pedagogical terms, an over-emphasis in language teaching on single words out of context may leave second language learners ill-prepared both in terms of the processing of heavily-chunked input such as casual conversation, as well as in terms of productive fluency. Wray, whose recent work on what she calls *formulaic sequences* (which include idioms, collocations and institutionalized sentence frames), stresses that both formally and functionally, formulaic sequences circumvent the analytical processes associated with the interpretation of open syntactic frames in terms of both encoding and decoding (see Wray 2000, 2002). She also notes, with relevance to the present paper, that utterances may be formulaic 'even though they do not need to be' (Wray 2000: 466), in the sense that they can be generated by the rules of open syntax and the lexicon (she gives as an example *It was lovely to see you*). Their formulaic nature resides in their recurrence and established lexico-grammatical patterns in alliance with their pragmatically specialized functions (in the case of *it was lovely to see you,* a follow-up message after spending pleasurable time with someone).

The present paper attempts to shift the balance away from the more semantically opaque multi-word expressions and seeks to tease out some of the most common sequences in everyday talk. As with most high-frequency phenomena, their recurrence is typically subliminal and not immediately accessible to the intuition of the native speaker. This paper therefore allows the first steps in the process of examining recurrent everyday multi-word strings to be effected automatically, by a computer count of recurring characters and spaces. This has both advantages and disadvantages, as the next section will show.

Data and method for the present study

Data and analytical procedure

This paper uses the 5-million word CANCODE spoken corpus. CANCODE stands for 'Cambridge and Nottingham Corpus of Discourse in English'. The corpus was established at the Department of English Studies, University of Nottingham, and is funded by Cambridge University Press. The corpus consists of five million words of transcribed conversations. The corpus recordings were made non-surreptitiously in a variety of settings including private homes, shops, offices and other public places, in non-formal settings across the islands of Britain and Ireland, with a wide demographic spread. The CANCODE corpus forms part of the larger Cambridge International Corpus. For further details of the CANCODE corpus and its construction, see McCarthy (1998).

The analytical software used for the present paper (Wordsmith Tools, Scott 1999) is capable of automatically retrieving recurrent strings of characters and spaces (words for our intents and purposes) and giving a count for their occurrence. The user sets the number of words for the recurrent strings (e.g., two-word strings, three-word strings) and any cut-off points for frequency (e.g., minimum 10/50/100 occurrences). This necessarily means that the software will retrieve strings which in many cases lack any syntactic or semantic integrity, as well as strings that display integrity of one or both kinds.

Computers in their present state cannot distinguish between strings which recur but which have no psychological status as units of meaning (e.g., the fragmentary string *to me and* occurs more than 100 times in the CANCODE corpus) and those units which have a semantic unity and syntactic integrity, even though they may be less frequent (e.g., the discourse-marker phrase *as far as I know* occurs with less than half the frequency of *to me and*). This difficulty has led some researchers (e.g., Altenberg 1998; De Cock 2000) to incorporate fragmentary strings into their definition of chunks even where these include sub-phrasal and sub-clausal strings (De Cock offers as examples *in the* and *that the*), alongside pragmatically adequate sentence-frames such as *it is true that*. In the present paper we wish to focus on those items in the automatically extracted strings which display pragmatic integrity regardless of their syntax or lack of semantic wholeness, a task which necessitates manual inferencing and interpretation of the automatically generated data (see below).

The procedure for extracting the recurrent strings was to generate rank-order frequency lists of two-, three-, four-, five-, and six-word sequences for the entire 5-million word corpus. For practical reasons, a frequency cut-off point had to be established, and for the present purposes, an occurrence of at least 4 times per million words was the criterion for inclusion (in other words 20 times in the 5-million word corpus). This compares with Biber et al's (1999) figure of 10 times per million and Cortes' (2002) figure of 20 per million. Our figure is more liberal mainly because of the low occurrence of six-word clusters (only 18 being generated at the necessary 20 or more occurrences in five million words). Six-word recurrent clusters are of very low frequency in CANCODE, and it does seem that six is a practical cut-off point beyond which recurrent clusters seem to be extremely rare. Only one cluster of seven words occurs more than 20 times: *but at the end of the day* (on the 'magic' number of seven as a psychological limit, see Miller, 1956). The lists for the smaller combinations were, predictably, much longer. Figure 1 shows the comparative distribution of two-, three-, four-, five-, and six-word clusters in excess of 20 occurrences, and it can be seen that there is a very sharp fall-off between three-word clusters and four-word clusters, and an even sharper drop between four- and five-word clusters. It should be noted that, in these counts, contracted forms such as *it's* and *don't* are considered as one 'word', since the computer is counting characters and spaces only.

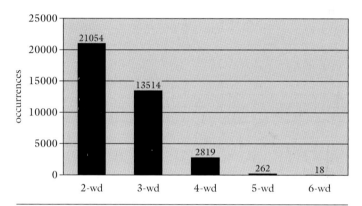

Figure 1: Distribution of clusters in excess of 20 occurrences

Results

Tables 1 to 5 show the top 20 items in each cluster list for 2–5 word clusters, and all of the 6-word clusters.

	Word	Freq.
1	YOU KNOW	28,013
2	I MEAN	17,158
3	I THINK	14,086
4	IN THE	13,887
5	IT WAS	12,608
6	I DON'T	11,975
7	OF THE	11,048
8	AND I	9,722
9	SORT OF	9,586
10	DO YOU	9,164
11	I WAS	8,174
12	ON THE	8,136
13	AND THEN	7,733
14	TO BE	7,165
15	IF YOU	6,709
16	DON'T KNOW	6,614
17	TO THE	6,157
18	AT THE	6,029
19	HAVE TO	5,914
20	YOU CAN	5,828

Table 1: Top 20 two-word clusters

	Word	Freq.
1	I DON'T KNOW	5,308
2	A LOT OF	2,872
3	I MEAN I	2,186
4	I DON'T THINK	2,174
5	DO YOU THINK	1,511
6	DO YOU WANT	1,426
7	ONE OF THE	1,332
8	YOU HAVE TO	1,300
9	IT WAS A	1,273
10	YOU KNOW I	1,231
11	YOU WANT TO	1,230
12	YOU KNOW WHAT	1,212
13	DO YOU KNOW	1,203
14	A BIT OF	1,201
15	I THINK IT'S	1,189
16	BUT I MEAN	1,163
17	AND IT WAS	1,148
18	A COUPLE OF	1,136
19	YOU KNOW THE	1,079
20	WHAT DO YOU	1,065

Table 2: Top 20 three-word clusters

	Word	Freq.
1	YOU KNOW WHAT I	680
2	KNOW WHAT I MEAN	674
3	I DON'T KNOW WHAT	513
4	THE END OF THE	512
5	AT THE END OF	508
6	DO YOU WANT TO	483
7	A BIT OF A	457
8	DO YOU KNOW WHAT	393
9	I DON'T KNOW IF	390
10	I THINK IT WAS	372
11	A LOT OF PEOPLE	350
12	THANK YOU VERY MUCH	343
13	I DON'T KNOW WHETHER	335
14	AND THINGS LIKE THAT	329
15	OR SOMETHING LIKE THAT	328
16	WHAT DO YOU THINK	312
17	I THOUGHT IT WAS	303
18	I DON'T WANT TO	296
19	THAT SORT OF THING	294
20	YOU KNOW I MEAN	294

Table 3: Top 20 four-word clusters

	Word	Freq.
1	YOU KNOW WHAT I MEAN	639
2	AT THE END OF THE	332
3	DO YOU KNOW WHAT I	258
4	THE END OF THE DAY	235
5	DO YOU WANT ME TO	177
6	IN THE MIDDLE OF THE	102
7	I MEAN I DON'T KNOW	94
8	THIS THAT AND THE OTHER	88
9	I KNOW WHAT YOU MEAN	84
10	ALL THE REST OF IT	76
11	AND ALL THAT SORT OF	74
12	I WAS GOING TO SAY	71
13	AND ALL THE REST OF	68
14	AND THAT SORT OF THING	68
15	I DON'T KNOW WHAT IT	63
16	ALL THAT SORT OF THING	61
17	DO YOU WANT TO GO	61
18	TO BE HONEST WITH YOU	59
19	AN HOUR AND A HALF	56
20	IT'S A BIT OF A	56

Table 4: Top 20 five-word clusters

	Word	Freq.
1	DO YOU KNOW WHAT I MEAN	236
2	AT THE END OF THE DAY	222
3	AND ALL THE REST OF IT	64
4	AND ALL THAT SORT OF THING	41
5	I DON'T KNOW WHAT IT IS	38
6	BUT AT THE END OF THE	35
7	AND THIS THAT AND THE OTHER	33
8	FROM THE POINT OF VIEW OF	33
9	A HELL OF A LOT OF	29
10	IN THE MIDDLE OF THE NIGHT	29
11	DO YOU WANT ME TO DO	24
12	ON THE OTHER SIDE OF THE	24
13	I DON'T KNOW WHAT TO DO	23
14	AND ALL THIS SORT OF THING	22
15	AND AT THE END OF THE	22
16	IF YOU SEE WHAT I MEAN	22
17	DO YOU WANT TO HAVE A	21
18	IF YOU KNOW WHAT I MEAN	21

Table 5: The six-word clusters (all)

The tables exclude repetitions such as *you, you, you,* which often occur as stutter starts (although we recognize that these may indeed have importance in some kinds of analysis) and non-lexical phenomena such as hesitation markers (e.g., *er, er*). The lists were then used as the basis for analysis and interpretation, firstly in terms of identifying integrated units, and then in terms of what such units reveal about conversational interaction.

Clusters and single words

It is useful to gain a perspective on how the high frequency clusters relate to the distribution of single words in the corpus. An exhaustive count is beyond the scope of this paper, but some indicative examples are offered to assist the overall understanding of the place of clusters in a corpus-based description of the lexicon.

Only 33 items in the single-word rank order frequency list for CANCODE occur more frequently than the most frequent cluster (i.e., more frequently than the number one *you know,* which occurs 28,013 times). Clearly then, *you know* is one of the most frequent items in the English lexicon.

A selection of two-word clusters which occur with greater frequency than some common, everyday single words is given in Figure 2.

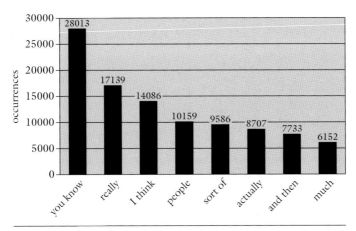

Figure 2: Two-word clusters and common single words

Individual clusters will be commented on below. Figure 3 below shows examples of three- and four-word clusters which occur more frequently than some common everyday words.

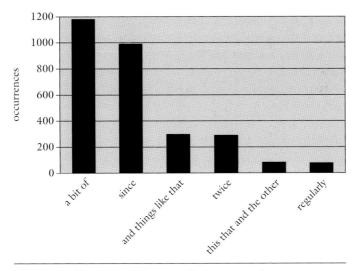

Figure 3: Three- and four-word clusters and common single words

The graphs suggest that word lists which focus only on single words risk losing sight of the fact that many high-frequency clusters are more frequent and central to communication than even very frequent words. However, the question remains whether the clusters in the tables and figures presented here should be considered as units of any kind or simply as statistical phenomena reflecting inevitable recurrence of a finite number of words in the vocabulary. In short, should something like *and then* be merely viewed as a co-occurrence arising from the extremely high frequency and weak collocability of its component words and their inevitable repeated collision in the corpus, or do such co-occurrences reveal anything about how we converse with one another?

Clusters as units of interaction

Pragmatic integrity

Many of the recurrent clusters present in the tables and graphs above are syntactic fragments, i.e., they do not constitute complete syntactic elements at phrasal or clausal levels. These include *in the, and I, of the* and *do you* in the two-word list; *one of the* and *I think it's* in the three-word list; *the end of the* and *a bit of a* in the four-word list; and so on. Conventional grammars would certainly label these as incomplete in terms of structural units. That is not to say that all models of grammar would reject such phenomena: emergent grammar, as epitomized in the work of Hopper (1998), considers fragments to be important clues as to how interaction unfolds and how meaning emerges rather than being pre-determined in linguistic units. And there is no obvious reason why one should exclude syntactically fragmentary strings from consideration when evaluating their *interactive* role. For instance, *I think it's* is indicative of the ubiquity of *I think* as a hedge prefacing evaluations of situations likely to be referred to by pro-form *it*. *I think* is number 3 in the two-word list, occurring more than 14,000 times. *A bit of a* may be considered similarly: speakers routinely downtone utterances with *a bit (of a)* (e.g., *it's a bit late, it was a bit of a mess*), evidenced by the fact that *a bit* occupies rank number 24 (with a frequency of 5,341) in the two-word cluster list. Thus although an expression like *a bit* may be semantically delexicalized (in other words fairly lexically 'empty'), and although it may be syntactically dependent in its role as a modifier, it is pragmatically specialized as a downtoner, and exhibits pragmatic adequacy and integrity. Other clusters seem less pragmatically motivated (e.g., *it was, what do you, in the middle of the*) and their occurrence is probably due to the regularity and stability of the content-world itself. For example, the cluster *an hour and a half* is number 19 in the five-word list; this may simply reflect the fact that people frequently make references to time and duration. We would argue, then, that it is in pragmatic categories rather than syntactic or semantic ones that we are likely to find the reasons why many of the strings of words are so recurrent. By pragmatic categories here we mean those which embrace the creation of speaker meanings in context. Such categories include discourse marking, the preservation of face and the expression of politeness, and the acts of hedging and purposive vagueness, all of which create the speaker-listener world rather than the content- or propositional world.

Discourse marking

Some of the most frequent clusters have discourse-marking functions. These include:

>*You know*
>*I mean*
>*And then*
>*But I mean*
>*You know what I mean*
>*Do you know what I mean*
>*At the end of the day*
>*If you see what I mean*

You know, as the most frequent cluster of all, is an important token of projected shared knowledge between speaker and listener, as well as being a topic-launcher (Östman 1981; Erman 1987); it is ubiquitous in everyday informal talk, as extract (1) shows:

[All corpus extracts indicate the different speakers as <$1>, <$2>, etc. The equals sign (=) indicates a truncated word or turn. The plus sign (+) indicates that an incomplete turn continues after an interruption by another speaker.]

> (1)
> <$1> **You know**, our Gregory he's only fifteen but he wants to be a pilot.
> <$2> Does he?
> <$1> Now he couldn't get in this year to go to Manchester, **you know**, on that erm course that they do, experience course thing.
> <$2> Work experience.
> <$1> But he's going for next we= next year.
> <$2> Oh yeah.
> <$1> Work+
> <$3> Oh yeah.
> <$1> +experience yeah. And this time he's been to erm Headingley, coaching, doing a bit of coaching with the young kids **you know**.

The extended clusters *(do) you know what I mean* have a similar function of checking shared knowledge. Separately, *I mean* is used when shared knowledge is not inferred or when the speaker needs to reformulate (Erman 1987):

> (2)
> [In a sports equipment shop]
> <$1> Are there any tennis racquets you'd recommend? Erm I need the medium price range.

<$2> Medium price.

<$1> Yeah.

<$2> What are you looking= What sort of price range are you look-
ing at?

<$1> Erm well not too expensive.

<$2> **I mean**, they start at m= about fifteen pounds and they go up
anywhere to about three hundred quid.

<$1> Oh right. Probably under a hundred pounds cos it's not+

<$2> Okay.

<$1> +professional.

<$2> Is it for yourself?

<$1> Yeah.

<$2> **I mean**, the decent racquets, you've got you've got a Head
seventy nine.

<$1> Yeah.

The overlap of components within *(do) you know (what) (I mean)*
partly account for the extreme high frequency of *you know* and *I mean*, but
above all it is their core function in the monitoring of the state of shared
knowledge which gives them the pragmatic integrity which qualifies them for
consideration as units. Likewise, *and then* is extremely frequent in narrative as
a marker of temporal sequence, while *at the end of the day* typically has a sum-
marizing function.

Face and politeness

Speakers use indirect forms to perform speech acts such as directives and
requests in order to protect the face of their receivers, and the clusters reveal
common everyday frames for such acts. Indirectness is also important in the
polite and non-face-threatening expression of attitude, opinion, and stance.
Speakers work hard to protect the face of their interlocutors, wishing neither to
demean them or coerce them (See Brown and Levinson 1987). Clusters in this
category include:

> *Do you think*
> *Do you want (me) (to)*
> *I don't know if/whether*
> *What do you think*
> *I was going to say*

Extracts (3) and (4) show these in action:

(3)

[Discussing the priorities for preserving lives in the British National Health Service, and whether age should be a factor]

<$2> I thought it was shocking.

<$1> Mm. **Do you think it** would have made any difference if she was say eighty years of age instead of a teenager?

<$2> Well I think that er anyone's attitude should be to save life irrespective of age

(4)

[At a travel agent's]

<$3> Did you want to take out insurance?

<$1> Erm I'd like to ask about it but **I don't know if** I want to do that today.

<$3> Okay.

The utterances containing the clusters can be perfectly well-formed with more direct assertions (e.g., *Would it have made any difference . . . ?; I don't want to do that today*) but the presence of the clusters plays a significant role in the mutual protection of face and the smooth, sensitive, and polite progression of the talk. Once again, it is pragmatic integrity rather than syntactic or semantic wholeness which is most relevant.

Another important aspect of face-protection and politeness is hedging. Some of the most frequent clusters have a hedging function, i.e., they modify propositions to make them less assertive and less open to challenge or refutation. These include:

> *I think*
> *Sort of*
> *A bit (of a)*
> *I don't know*
> *I don't think*
> *To be honest with you*

Extracts (5) and (6) illustrate these functions.

(5)

<$1> That's fine Jess. Are there many to do?

<$2> No.

<$1> No. I've got an appointment in Healdham at five fifty so I'm going to have to leave you know **sort of** shortly after three.

(6)

<$1> I went to college in the spring

<$2> Mm.

<$2> and sat the exam in June and passed it.

<$1> Mm.

<$2> But it was basically er an E-E-C update on the new regulations. **To be honest with you** it was pret= pretty easy I thought but you know s= some people have to fail I suppose and some do it you know.

Vagueness and approximation

Equally apparent in the high frequency clusters are markers of purposive vagueness and approximation. Vagueness is central to informal conversation, and its absence can make utterances blunt and pedantic, especially in such domains as references to number and quantity, where approximations are the norm in conversation. Vagueness also enables speakers to refer to semantic categories in an open-ended way which calls on shared cultural and real-world knowledge to fill in the category members referred to only obliquely (see Chafe 1982; Powell 1985; Channell 1994). Such tokens include:

> *A couple of*
> *And things like that*
> *Or something like that*
> *(And) that sort of thing*
> *(And) this that and the other*
> *All the rest of it*
> *(And) all this/that sort of thing*

Examples from the corpus show the clusters in action.

(7)

[At a travel agent's]

<$1> And what about er local taxis **and things like that**? Are they included or are they extra?

<$2> Er everything is included apart from any sort of top up insurance you may want.

(8)

<$1> She said, "We've just come out here. We've just bought an apartment here."

<$2> Mm.

<$1> And she said, "We've come out to furnish it and buy the furniture **and this that and the other**."

In extracts (7) and (8) it would be clearly conversationally inappropriate to list all the items implied by the vague tokens; speakers need only allude to the shared cultural knowledge and may assume their listeners can fill in the detail. Once again, the vague tokens exhibit pragmatic integrity and play central interactive roles, even though their syntax is incomplete and dependent.

Discussion and conclusion

Not all of the clusters can or need to be accounted for in terms of pragmatic integrity. For example, clusters such as *on the, it was a,* and so on are probably best explained either by their semantics (e.g., core spatio-temporal notions) and by the frequency of acts such as describing location or narrating the past. However, by exploring the uses of the clusters in the corpus, it does seem that amongst the most frequent (the top 20 in each case), there seem to be a considerable number which achieve wholeness as units when their pragmatic functions are adduced. What such clusters show is the all-pervasiveness of inter-active meanings in everyday conversation and the degree to which speakers constantly engage on the interactive plane as well as the transactional or content plane. Their addition to the vocabulary list of any language is not an optional extra, since the meanings they create are extremely frequent and necessary in discourse, and are fundamental to successful interaction. The units support Sinclair's notion of the idiom principle at work, with the clusters best viewed as being evidence of single linguistic choices rather than assembled at the moment of speaking. They make fluency a reality.

A final word needs to be said about the status of such units vis-à-vis the more opaque idiomatic units that have traditionally been studied. In the absence of corpus evidence it is difficult to introspect on what one says. It is much easier to introspect on what one writes, and additionally, introspection is more likely to light upon the colourful, the curious, the rare, precisely because such items are psychologically salient. Hence it should not surprise us that, with few exceptions, pre-corpus studies of multi-word units focussed on idioms, phrasal verbs, compounds, and so on, either as colourful curiosities or, in the pedagogic domain, a difficult characteristic of English for learners to struggle with. Meanwhile the banal, hidden, subliminal patterns of the everyday lexicon stubbornly resisted exposure. Corpus analysis enables us to circumvent our dif-ficulties in retrieving such patterned occurrences, but the automatic retrieval of recurrent strings is only the beginning, and a good deal of inferential analysis is still necessary to see meaning in the mechanical and dispassionate statistics spewed out by the computer.

References

Aisenstadt, Esther. 1981. Restricted collocations in English lexicology and lexicography. *ITL Review of Applied Linguistics* 53: 53-61.

Altenberg, Bengt. 1998. On the phraseology of spoken English: the evidence of recurrent word combinations. *Phraseology: Theory Analysis and Applications,* ed. by Anthony Cowie, 101-122. Oxford: Oxford University Press.

Bazell, Charles, John Catford, Michael Halliday, and Robert Robins, eds. 1966. *In Memory of J. R. Firth.* London: Longman.

Benson, Morton and Evelyn Benson. 1993. *Russian-English Dictionary of Verbal Collocations (REDVC).* Amsterdam: Benjamins.

Biber, Douglas and Susan Conrad. 1999. Lexical bundles in conversation and academic prose. *Out of Corpora: Studies in Honor of Stig Johansson,* ed. by Hilde Hasselgard and Signe Oksefjell, 181-190. Amsterdam: Rodopi.

Biber, Douglas, Stig Johansson, Geoffrey Leech, Susan Conrad and Edward Finegan. 1999. *Longman Grammar of Spoken and Written English.* London: Longman.

Bolinger, Dwight. 1976. Meaning and memory. *Forum Linguisticum,* 1: 1-14.

Brown, Penelope and Stephen Levinson. 1987. *Politeness: Some Universals in Language Usage.* Cambridge: Cambridge University Press.

Chafe, Wallace. 1982. Integration and involvement in speaking, writing, and oral literature. *Spoken and Written Language: Exploring Orality and Literacy,* ed. by Deborah Tannen, 35-53. Norwood, N.J.: Ablex Publishing Corporation.

Channell, Joanna. 1994. *Vague Language.* Oxford: Oxford University Press.

Chomsky, Noam. 1965. *Aspects of the Theory of Syntax.* Cambridge, MA: MIT Press.

Cortes, Viviana. 2002. Lexical bundles in freshman composition. In Reppen et al. 131-145.

Coulmas, Florian. 1979. On the sociolinguistic relevance of routine formulae. *Journal of Pragmatics* 3: 239-66.

Coulmas, Florian, ed. 1981a. *Conversational Routine.* The Hague: Mouton.

Coulmas, Florian. 1981b. Idiomaticity as a problem of pragmatics. *Possibilities and Limitations of Pragmatics,* ed. by Herman Parret, Marina Sbisà, and Jef Verschueren, 139-51. Amsterdam: John Benjamins.

Cowie, Anthony. 1988. Stable and creative aspects of vocabulary use. *Vocabulary and Language Teaching,* ed. By Ronald Carter and Michael McCarthy, 126-39. London: Longman.

De Cock, Sylvie. 1998. A recurrent word combination approach to the study of formulae in the speech of native and non-native speakers of English. *International Journal of Corpus Linguistics* 3: 59-80.

De Cock, Sylvie. 2000. Repetitive phrasal chunkiness and advanced EFL speech and writing. *Corpus Linguistics and Linguistic Theory. Papers from ICAME 20 1999*, ed. by Christian Mair and Marianne Hundt, 51-68. Amsterdam: Rodopi.

Drew, Paul and Elizabeth Holt. 1998. Figures of speech: figurative expressions and the management of topic transition in conversation. *Language in Society* 27: 495-522.

Erman, Britt. 1987. *Pragmatic Expressions in English: A Study of "you know," "you see," and "I mean" in Face-to-face Conversation*. Stockholm: Almqvist & Wiksell.

Fernando, Chitra and Roger Flavell. 1981. *On Idiom: Critical Views and Perspectives*. Exeter: University of Exeter.

Firth, John Rupert. 1935. The technique of semantics. *Transactions of the Philological Society.* 36-72.

Firth, John Rupert. 1951/1957. *Papers in Linguistics*. Oxford: Oxford University Press, 190-215.

Granger, Sylviane. 1998. Prefabricated writing patterns in advanced EFL writing: collocations and formulae. *Phraseology: Theory, Analysis and Applications,* ed. by Anthony Cowie, 145-160. Oxford: Clarendon Press.

Hakuta, Kenji. 1974. Prefabricated patterns and the emergence of structure in second language acquisition. *Language Learning* 24: 287-298.

Halliday, Michael. 1966. Lexis as a linguistic level. In Bazell, et al. (1966) 148-162.

Hopper, Paul. 1998. Emergent Grammar, *The New Psychology of Language,* ed. by Michael Tomasello, 155-175. Hillsdale NJ: Lawrence Erlbaum Associates.

Howarth, Peter. 1998. Phraseology and Second Language Proficiency. *Applied Linguistics* 19 (1): 24-44.

Kunin, Aleksandr. 1970. *Anglijskasa frazeologija*. Moscow: Izdat'elstvo 'Vysšajaškola'.

Lewis, Michael. 1993. *The Lexical Approach: The State of ELT and a Way Forward*. Hove UK: LTP.

Makkai, Adam. 1978. Idiomaticity as a language universal. *Universals of Human Language, Volume 3: Word Structure,* ed. by Joseph Greenberg, 401-448. Stanford, CA: Stanford University Press.

McCarthy, Michael. 1998. *Spoken Language and Applied Linguistics*. Cambridge: Cambridge University Press.

Miller, George. 1956. The magical number seven, plus or minus two: some limits on our capacity for processing information. *Psychological Review* 63: 81-97.

Mitchell, Terence. 1971. Linguistic 'goings-on': collocations and other lexical matters arising on the linguistic record. *Archivum Linguisticum* 2: 35-69.

Nattinger, James and Jeaneete DeCarrico. 1992. *Lexical Phrases and Language Teaching*. Oxford: Oxford University Press.

Oakey, David. 2002. Formulaic language in English academic writing. In Reppen et al., 111-129. Amsterdam: John Benjamins.

Östman, Jan-Ola. 1981. *You Know: A Discourse Functional Approach*. Amsterdam: John Benjamins.

Pawley, Andrew and Frances Syder. 1983. Two puzzles for linguistic theory: nativelike selection and nativelike fluency. *Language and Communication*, ed. by Jack Richards and Richard Schmidt, 191-226. New York: Longman.

Powell, Mava. 1985. Purposeful vagueness: an evaluative dimension of vague quantifying expressions. *Journal of Linguistics* 21: 31-50.

Powell, Mava. 1992. Semantic/pragmatic regularities in informal lexis: British speakers in spontaneous conversational settings. *Text* 12 (1): 19-58.

Reppen, Randi, Susan Fitzmaurice and Douglas Biber, eds. 2002. *Using Corpora to Explore Linguistic Variation*. Amsterdam: John Benjamins.

Scott, Michael. 1999. *Wordsmith Tools*. Software. Oxford: Oxford University Press.

Sinclair, John. 1966. Beginning the study of lexis. In Bazell et al., 410-430. London: Longman.

Sinclair, John. 1987. Collocation: a progress report. In Steele and Threadgold (1987), 319-331.

Sinclair, John. 1991. *Corpus, Concordance, Collocation*. Oxford: Oxford University Press.

Sinclair, John. 1996. The search for the units of meaning. *Textus* IX: 75-106.

Steele, Ross and Terry Threadgold, eds. 1987. *Language Topics: An International Collection of Papers by Colleagues, Students and Admirers of Professor Michael Halliday to Honour him on his Retirement*, Vol. II. Amsterdam: John Benjamins.

Strässler, Jörg. 1982. *Idioms in English: a Pragmatic Analysis*. Tübingen: Gunter Narr Verlag.

Wray, Alison. 2000. Formulaic sequences in second language teaching: principle and practice. *Applied Linguistics*, 21 (4): 463-489.

Wray, Alison. 2002. *Formulaic Language and the Lexicon*. Cambridge: Cambridge University Press.

3 | *Ten criteria for a spoken grammar*[1]

Reprinted with Permission: *New Perspectives on Grammar Teaching in Second Language*, LEA, Inc. pp. 51-75.

Michael McCarthy and Ronald Carter
University of Nottingham, UK

Abstract

In "Ten Criteria for a Spoken Grammar," Michael McCarthy and Ronald Carter discuss how corpus analysis reveals important differences between spoken and written grammar in the English language. They identify ten principles of special importance in the development of a spoken grammar.

1. **Establish core units of a spoken grammar**
   Many basic structures of spoken English do not conform to the norms of written language. The nature of some of these structures is examined.

2. **Phrasal complexity**
   In contrast to deterministic and behavioristic grammars, probabilistic grammar considers what forms of language are *likely* to occur in general usage and concerns itself with "factual utterances" rather than with "correct sentences." This approach gives legitimacy to a greater range of phrasal complexity than traditional approaches have allowed.

3. **Tense, voice, aspect, and interpersonal and textual meaning**
   Grammatical formations are often influenced by such interpersonal concerns as the relationship between the speaker/writer and the listener/reader. Particularly in spoken exchanges, tentativeness, indirectness, and politeness frequently influence grammatical choices. Speakers sometimes choose tense and aspect to shape their narrative style rather than to establish temporal references, per se.

4. **Position of clause elements**
   Corpus analysis reveals that spoken English is more flexible than written English in respect to the variety of choices that speakers enjoy when positioning clause elements in sentences.

---

1 The editors would like to thank Cambridge University Press for permission to cite examples from their corpus.

5. **Clause complexes**

The nature of clause complexes in spoken English is examined. Clauses introduced by *which* and *because* – traditionally restricted to a subordinate function – are shown to have the capacity to function as main clauses as well.

6. **Unpleasant anomalies**

In constructing a probabilistic grammar, long-held beliefs of correct usage must sometimes be abandoned. Double negatives and the use of "would" in conditional clauses – traditionally proscribed – are shown to be sometimes admissible in spoken English.

7. **Larger sequences**

Grammatical sequences are demonstrated to exist across longer stretches of text than have traditionally been examined. The grammarian must therefore begin to think in terms of discourse grammar, looking beyond the boundaries of isolated sentences and across speaker turns to observe extended patterns.

8. **The comparative criterion**

The existence of substantial commonality between spoken and written forms points to the need for a single grammar that can accommodate both. The observation that spoken forms have a strong influence on popular writing (in tabloid journals, e-mail, advertisements, etc.) is presented as evidence of the blurred distinction between written and spoken forms.

9. **Metalanguage**

The terminology that has traditionally been used to describe grammar developed from the classification of written forms. Existing metalanguage cannot always cope with spoken data and tends to treat it as abnormal. The authors propose that a metalanguage adequate to describe both written and spoken grammatical forms should therefore be devised.

10. **Native and non-native users**

The question of grammatical authority is raised. The status of regional dialects and non-native English is examined in the context of building representative corpora.

Introduction

In recent articles and books, we have reported some of the findings of our research into the grammatical characteristics of the five-million-word CANCODE (Cambridge and Nottingham Corpus of Discourse of English) spoken corpus (Carter & McCarthy, 1995a, 1955b, 1997; Carter, Hughes & McCarthy, 1998; Hughes & McCarthy, 1998; McCarthy, 1998). Although these works have tended to focus on specific aspects of spoken grammars, a common thread unites them: the belief that spoken grammars have uniquely special qualities that distinguish them from written ones, wherever we look in our corpus, at whatever level of grammatical category. In our work, too, we have expressed the view that language pedagogy that claims to support the teaching and learning of speaking skills does itself a disservice if it ignores what we know about the spoken language. Whatever else may be the result of imaginative methodologies for eliciting spoken language in the second-language classroom, there can be little hope for a natural spoken output on the part of language learners if the input is stubbornly rooted in models that owe their origin and shape to the written language. Even much corpus-based grammatical insight (for example, the otherwise excellent early products of the University of Birmingham COBUILD corpus project) has been heavily biased towards evidence gleaned from written sources. Therefore, we believe it is timely to consider some of the insights a spoken corpus can offer, and to attempt to relate them more globally to the overall problem of designing a pedagogical spoken grammar. We do this in the form of 10 principles that might inform any spoken grammar project, and which, we feel, give us a distinct purchase on this relatively recent area of pedagogical interest[2]. Each of the 10 principles will be exemplified with extracts from the CANCODE spoken corpus. CANCODE was established at the Department of English Studies, University of Nottingham, United Kingdom, and is funded by Cambridge University Press, with whom the sole copyright resides. The corpus consists of five million words of transcribed conversations. The corpus tape recordings were made in a variety of settings including private homes, shops, offices and other public places, and educational institutions (though informal settings) across the islands of Britain and Ireland, with a wide demographic spread. For further details of the corpus and its construction, see McCarthy (1998).

---

2 Although we claim that widespread interest in spoken grammars is recent, we do not wish to dismiss the pioneering work of grammarians such as Palmer and Blandford (1969), who were way ahead of their time in seeing what was important for a grammar of spoken language (for examples and a brief discussion, see McCarthy, 1998, pp. 17–18). Early spoken grammars, however, did not have the benefit of large-scale computerized corpora, and it is this we refer to in our use of the words "relatively recent."

Establishing core units of a spoken grammar

Even a cursory glance at a conversational transcript immediately raises the problem of the frequent occurrence of units that do not conform to the notion of well-formed "sentences" with main and subordinate clauses (see Lerner, 1991). Conversational turns often consist just of phrases, or of incomplete clauses, or of clauses with subordinate clause characteristics but that are apparently not attached to any main clause, and so forth. Hockett (1986) pertinently notes that linguists have tended to ignore such phenomena, but "speakers and hearers do not ignore them—they carry a sizeable share of the communicative load." Example 1 shows some of the kinds of units frequently encountered in a spoken corpus. Problematic areas for a traditional grammar, here and in following examples, are printed in italic type:

Example 1

Speakers are sitting at the dinner table talking about a car accident that happened to the father of one of the speakers.

Speaker 1: I'll just take that off. *Take that off.*
Speaker 2: *All looks great.*
Speaker 3: [laughs]
Speaker 2: Mm.
Speaker 3: Mm.
Speaker 2: I think your dad was amazed wasn't he at the damage.
Speaker 4: Mm.
Speaker 2: It's not so much the parts. It's the labour charges for
Speaker 4: *Oh that. For a car.*
Speaker 2: Have you got hold of it?
Speaker 1: Yeah.
Speaker 2: *It was a bit erm.*
Speaker 1: Mm.
Speaker 3: Mm.
Speaker 2: *A bit.*
Speaker 3: That's right.
Speaker 2: I mean they said they'd have to take his car in for two days. And he says All it is is s= straightening a panel. *And they're like,* Oh no. It's all new panel. You can't do this.
Speaker 3: *Any erm problem.*
Speaker 2: *As soon as they hear insurance claim.* Oh. Let's get it right.
Speaker 3: Yeah. Yeah. *Anything to do with+*

Speaker 1: *Yow.*
Speaker 3: *+coach work is er+*
Speaker 1: Right.
Speaker 3: *+fatal isn't it.*
Speaker 1: *Now.*

Here we may observe the following phenomena:

1. Indeterminate structures (is the second *Take that off* an ellipted form of *I'll just take that off*? Is it an imperative? Is *All looks great* well formed? What is the status of *And they're like*?)

2. Phrasal utterances, communicatively complete in themselves, but not sentences (*Oh that. For a car. Any problem.*)

3. Aborted or incomplete structures (*It was a bit erm . . . A bit.*)

4. "Subordinate" clauses not obviously connected to any particular main clause (*As soon as they hear insurance claim.*)

5. Interrupted structures with other speaker contributions intervening (*Anything to do with . . . coach work is er . . . fatal isn't it.*)

6. Words of unclear grammatical class (*Yow. Now.*)

An even more complex question arises with *joint-production* grammatical units; that is to say, when a grammatical unit is complete only when a second participant adds his or her contribution, as in Example 2.

Example 2

[Customer and waiter in restaurant:]
Customer: Yeah. *Let's just have er*
Waiter: *Some rice?*
Customer: Yeah.

These phenomena, normal in everyday talk, raise questions about the nature of basic units and classes in a spoken grammar, and the solution would seem to be to raise the status of the word, phrase, and clause to that of (potentially) independent units; to recognize the potential for joint production of units; and to downplay the status of the sentence as the main target unit for communication. But the fact that well-formed sentences exist side by side with a variety of other types of units raises further questions, too, which include: What status does the traditional notion of SVO clause structure for a language like English have in conversational data? Are the "ellipted" utterances of conversation really just a reduced and partial form of the "real" grammar? Or are the well-formed sentences of written texts elaborated versions of the sparse and economical basic spoken structures, elaborated because they have less contextual support in writing and therefore necessarily must increase the amount of redundancy? There are by no means simple answers to these questions, but one's stance towards them can have major implications for what is considered correct or acceptable in a pedagogical grammar. If we accept the integrity of nonstandard units in a spoken grammar, then in general terms a spoken grammar is likely to be more liberal in what it accepts as "adequately formed," which itself may be preferable to the term "well-formed," with its connotations of native-speaker intuition. Native speakers, when asked to judge the grammaticality of decontextualized sentences, are more than likely to attempt a minimal contextualization (something akin to a written sentence), and their judgements may have no greater validity than that (i.e., that the sentence is grammatical or ungrammatical by written standards). Corpus evidence is different from intuitive judgements: It is not "in there" (internal, in the grammarian's or informant's head); rather it is "out there" (external, recorded as used, and preferably supported by widespread occurrences across a number of speakers). External evidence points us toward a socially embedded grammar, one with criteria for acceptability based on adequate communicability in real contexts, among real participants. It is evidence that cannot simply be dismissed as "ungrammatical."

Phrasal complexity

Pedagogical grammars generally describe the full structural complexity of any given unit (e.g., see Swan, 1995, p. 8 on the potential sequences of adjectives before noun heads), but significant differences may exist in the distribution of potential elements in actual discourse. The noun phrase is a good case in point. Although, in English, there is considerable potential for accumulating adjectives and noun modifiers before the head noun, this rarely in fact happens in everyday conversational data. If we take the noun *house* in headword position, for example, we find 1,379 occurrences of it in a 2.5-million-word sample of the CANCODE corpus. In these examples, where attributive adjectives occur, there is an overwhelming preference for simple determiner + one adjective + noun configurations, such as the following.

Examples 3 and 4

3. **Speaker 1:** Yeah it's *a big house*, six bedroom

4. **Speaker 1:** It's *a large house*, lovely, just right

The longest adjectival structure that occurs with *house* is: *Detached four-bedroomed house*. It will be noted, furthermore, in Examples 3 and 4, that further specification of the house is given in posthead appositional items (*six bedrooms* and *just right*). In a mixed written corpus sample of the same number of words, it is not difficult to find more complex adjectival configurations.

Examples 5 and 6

5. Living in *a big, dirty communal house* eating rubbish . . . (*The Guardian*, October 13, 1991, p. 16)

6. The *cozy lace-curtained* house . . . (*The Observer*, March 22, 1992, p. 22)

The point about these examples is not what can be said, but what is routinely said. Any speaker clearly may exercise the option to create a structurally complex noun phrase in ordinary conversation, but he or she will probably be heard as at best rather formal and at worst pedantic and bookish. However, a pedagogical issue of some importance arises here: If we label structures as *said* or *not said*, we run the risk of returning to the bad old days of behaviorism, describing behavior rather than the system of language that users employ. A partial solution lies in how we define *grammar*. A useful distinction can be made between deterministic grammar and probabilistic grammar. Deterministic grammar addresses structural prescription (e.g., that the past-tense morpheme in English is *-ed* rather than *-ing*, or that *the* precedes the noun rather than follows it). Determinism has served language teaching for centuries. Probabilistic grammar, on the other hand, considers what forms are most likely to be used in particular contexts, and the probabilities may be strong or weak. Itkonen (1980, p. 338) makes a distinction between "correct sentences" and "factually uttered sentences," and that is the direction we are also pursuing here. Probabilistic grammars by definition need real data to support their statements of probability, as well as analytical evaluation to get at the form-function relationships in particular contexts, from which usable probabilistic statements can then be constructed. Probabilistic grammar as a concept has been around for some time: Halliday (1961, p. 259) saw the basic nature of language as probabilistic and not as "always this and never that." He has in recent years refocused on this problem, with the help of corpus evidence. His concern is principally with how often the items in binary grammatical systems (e.g., present versus nonpresent) actually occur in relation to each other in real data. He concludes that the statistics of occurrence are "an essential property of the system—as essential as the terms of the opposition itself" (Halliday, 1991, p. 31). Halliday would acknowledge that a probabilistic statement such as "single-adjective noun phrases are *x* times more frequent in corpus A than in corpus B" does not necessarily have great predictive power, but he argues that it is important for interpreting the choice of form. Halliday (1992) supports our present position in arguing for the importance of examining different probabilities of occurrence in different registers, since it is unlikely that items in binary systemic opposition will be equiprobable in a corpus of any particular register. Halliday's disciples within the systemic-functional school of linguistics have further investigated unequal probabilities of occurrence of grammatical forms: For example, Nesbitt and Plum (1988) take a similar quantitative line in their research into the distribution of clause complexes. In our own published research (Carter and McCarthy, 1999), we have used grammatical probabilities to describe the occurrence of the English *get*-passive verb phrase (e.g., *He got killed,* in contrast to *He was killed*), which occurred 139 times in a 1.5-million-word sample of CANCODE spoken data. In our sample, 124 of the 139 examples referred in some way or another to what have been called "adversative" contexts (Chappell, 1980), that is, a state of affairs that is seen by the conversational participants as unfortunate, undesirable, or problematic. This is a strong probability, but does not preclude the occurrence of utterances such as *I got picked for the county,* which is newsworthy, but not "unfortunate" in its context (a tennis player describing the climb to success). Such "glad-tidings" examples, however, account for less than 5% of the relevant data. Equally interesting was the fact that 130 of the 139 *get*-passive examples had no agent explicitly stated, which is another case of a structural potential simply not being realized, in 93% of the recorded occurrences. We would argue that such probabilistic statements are in fact extremely useful in a pedagogical grammar; indeed, it is hard to envisage a proper description of the *get*-passive that would be pedagogically useful without including information for the learner about its overwhelming probability of occurrence in informal spoken contexts, with "unfortunate" events, and the unlikelihood of the occurrence of a typical passive *by*-agent phrase.

Thus, the issue of phrasal and other types of complexity and their different distribution in data may be subject to the principles of a probabilistic grammar, with the reminder that probabilities are not determinations, and that creative freedom and potential variation are always possible, in special circumstances, in order to avoid the grammar becoming overly-behavioristic.

Tense, voice, aspect, and interpersonal and textual meaning

Linguists have long recognized the different distributions of tense- and aspect-forms in different kinds of data. A good example of this is Waugh (1991), who looks at the distribution of the French *passé simple* (or preterite) form, which seems to be restricted to certain types of written text. One of the key factors, she asserts, is the concept of *detachment*: novels, stories, historical works, tales, legends, newspaper and magazine articles, and so forth (where the *passé simple* is most used) "are addressed to whom it may concern" (p. 243), in other words, an unnamed and only vaguely conceptualized recipient. It is this interpersonal consideration rather than the pastness of events per se that determines the use of the detached *passé simple* form; in conversation, the same events would normally be expressed with the "involving" present perfect tense form, projecting and reflecting a quite different set of participant relationships.

Waugh studied written data, but in spoken grammar, the fact that communication is face-to-face (or at least, in the case of phone talk, in real time to a real listener) clearly also affects grammatical choices that construct and reflect participant relationships. One such feature of the real-listener relationship is tentativeness and indirectness, a politeness strategy that minimizes imposition and threat to face (Brown & Levinson, 1987). This often manifests itself in tense and aspect choices that have traditionally been proscribed in pedagogical grammar, such as the use of progressive forms with verbs considered to be unamenable to progressive contexts, for example, *want, like, have to,* and so forth. Progressive forms of these verbs may indeed be rare or nonexistent in written data, but are by no means rare in spoken, as in Examples 7 and 8, in which the speakers seem to be adopting an indirect or non-assertive stance.

Examples 7 and 8

7. [Telephone inquiry to travel agent]
   Customer: Oh, hello, my husband and *I are wanting* to go to the Hook of Holland next weekend.

8. [Speakers in a business meeting]
   Speaker 1: So all of that. You see, when you devolve power as they did with the divisional structures, just all went off and did their own thing. And unfortunately *we're having to sort of come back* from that and say, well is that the most cost effective, because we've got to cut our costs.
   Speaker 2: Yeah.

Here, once again, we have a case for separating spoken and written grammar, and for making sure that our spoken grammar reflects the range of tense and aspect choices open to speakers to create appropriate interpersonal meanings.

The meanings created by tense and aspect choices may also be textually oriented. Such is often the case in oral narrative, in which speakers exercise considerable liberty in tense and aspect choice for the dramatization of events, or for their foregrounding and backgrounding. A considerable literature exists on tense and aspect in spoken narrative; for example, see Wolfson (1978, 1979) and Schiffrin (1981) for English. For other languages, see, for example, Silva-Coryvalán (1983) (Spanish), Soga (1983) (Japanese), and Paprotté (1988) (Greek). This is not to say that written narratives do not also exercise freedom with tense and aspect choices (see McCarthy, 1995, for some instances of this), but, once again, the distribution of such choices is different in the written and spoken modes, and the variation and rate of change from one form to another tends to be more intense in spoken narratives. Example 9 illustrates some of the typical spoken patterns:

Example 9

Speaker 1 is telling a story about how difficult it was to buy his favorite ice cream, called *Magnum,* in a small, provincial English town.

Speaker 1: So *we're looking* in there and *we can't find* any Magnums *so we turn round* and *he actually interrupts* his phone call to say you know what you looking for and *we said* have you got any Magnums [Speaker 2: Mm] and *he sort of shook his head* in a way as to say no you know we don't get such things it was a complete rejection [Speaker 3: Yeah] and we, *we sort of took a step* back from the thing and *there it was* labeled Magnum.

Such variation (here between simple past and so-called historic present) is by no means random or unmotivated, but coincides with important segments of the narrative, in which listeners are, as it were, taken in and out of the story-world in real time, as though they are participating in the drama themselves.

The point to be made here about spoken grammar is that a wide range of strategies is available to speakers to create and reinforce relationships and to involve or detach their listeners, and that the verb-phrase morphology plays a key role in signaling these functions. The pedagogical grammar of the spoken language must therefore ensure that the full functional range of choices is described and made available to learners, who should not be artificially restricted by proscriptive (and incomplete) rules based only on written data.

Voice is also more subtle and varied in the grammar of everyday conversation than most teaching materials would have learners think. There is, naturally, a focus on the core *be*-passive in contrast to the active voice. However, when we look at a large amount of conversational data we see that, as already noted in the section "Phrasal Complexity," the *get*-passive, massively more frequent in spoken data than in comparable amounts of written data, adds a further layer of choice, reflecting speakers' perceptions of good or bad fortune, or newsworthiness. In fact, the picture is even more complicated than that in spoken data, with the *be*- and straight *get*-passives of the type discussed in the section "Phrasal Complexity" forming just two points on a gradient or cline of passiveness that involves other *get*-constructions and *have* in a variety of configurations of agent and recipient roles (on the notion of a passive gradient in English, see Svartvik, 1966). Some examples follow.

Examples 10–16

10. You see, if ever you *get yourself locked out* . . .
11. Rian *got his nipple pierced* and it was so gross.
12. She *got me to do* a job for her, fencing.
13. Right we've got to *get you kitted out.*
14. The tape seems to have *got stuck.*
15. When the police came, they called a local garage and *had two recovery vehicles free my car.*
16. Our next-door neighbor's house was broken into again and he *had a few things stolen.*

Not only do Examples 10 to 16 display different syntactic patterns (e.g., reflexive and non-reflexive objects, presence or absence of infinitive *to*), but they also display different nuances of representation, with 10 suggesting some sort of responsibility on the part of the recipient, 14 being somewhat indeterminate as between an event and a state, 15 and 16 differing in terms of volition, and so forth. The clear lesson is that a spoken grammar will devote detailed attention to such complex phenomena, which might otherwise be underplayed in a grammar source only from written examples.

Position of clause elements

Pedagogical grammars naturally look for the most robust guidelines for the user, and rules about the positions of clause elements are extremely useful. The positions for adverbials are one such area where recurrent errors by learners are flagged and/or warned against. The *Collins*-COBUILD *English Grammar* (Collins-COBUILD, 1990, pp. 282–285), although stressing the flexibility of adverbial positioning in the clause, gives the basic positions as final, initial, and medial (between subject and verb), and a warning that, for some English-speakers, split infinitives (e.g., *To boldly go* . . .) are unacceptable. Eastwood (1994, p. 265) more directly warns against incorrect placement of adverbials between verb and direct object (e.g., *She speaks very well English.*). However, in certain spoken and written registers, most notably journalism, this latter "rule" is regularly contradicted in examples such as 17.

Example 17

Mr. [name] said he will fight *vigorously* attempts to extradite him to Britain. (BBC Radio 4 news, 3.8.98)

Moreover, in casual conversation in English, there is evidence that positioning is even more flexible, brought about by the exigencies of real-time synthesizing. For example, adverbials may occur after tags, and adverbs not normally considered amenable to final placement in written text regularly occur clause-finally.

Examples 18–21

18. Spanish is more widely used isn't it *outside of Europe?*

19. I was worried I was going to lose it and I did *almost.*

20. You know which one I mean *probably.*

21. [Speaker is talking about his job] It's a bit panicky but I've not got any deadlines like you have *though.*

The lesson here would seem to be that ordering of elements in the clause is likely to be different in spoken and written texts because of the real-time constraints of unrehearsed spoken language and the need for clear acts of topicalization and suchlike to appropriately orientate the listener. It is no surprise, therefore, that we find phenomena such as fronted objects to be much more frequent in conversation than in written texts, as well as emphatic placement of adverbials in first position.

Examples 22 and 23

22. *Those pipes* he said he's already disconnected; *the others* he's going to disconnect.

23. *The eighteenth* it starts.

Even more notable in spoken data, however, are the occasions when content matter is placed outside of the core clausal positions, in the form of what have traditionally been determined left- and right-displaced or left- and right-dislocated elements, or pre-posed and post-posed elements. Although left-dislocated elements are most typically single noun phrases, these can fulfill a variety of functions outside of the conventional clause structure.

Examples 24–28

24. *Paul,* in this job that he's got now, when *he* goes into the office *he's* never quite sure where he's going to be sent.

25. *A friend of mine, his* uncle had the taxi firm when we had the wedding.

26. *His cousin in Beccles, her boyfriend,* his parents bought *him* a Ford Escort for his birthday.

27. I mean typically, *an American,* you shake hands with an American, tell them your name and immediately they'll start using it.

28. Well, *this little story I was going to tell you about,* I was on holiday with an elderly friend of mine in Butlins, Barry Island, South Wales, as you know, and she asked me . . .

Examples 24 through 28 show that preplaced noun phrases can provide content for the subject (24), an attribute of the subject (25), or the object (26), can merely flag up an entity and repeat it in the upcoming clause (27), or can simply provide a broad topical framework not necessarily repeated in any subsequent element (28). Left-dislocated phenomena have been documented in a variety of languages (see, e.g., Aijmer, 1989; Geluykens, 1989, for English, French, and Italian; Geluykens, 1992, for English; Blasco, 1995, for French; Rivero, 1980, for Spanish), and it is clear that such choices reflect concern on the part of the speaker to bring the listener into the appropriate frame or schema for understanding the upcoming clause (often from a person or entity known to the listener to the new person or entity that is to be the topic). One only has to think how "unspeakable" and difficult to process similar clauses can be if uttered with the kinds of embedding often found in formal written styles (e.g., *His cousin in Beccles' boyfriend's parents bought him . . .*) to appreciate the naturalness of these phenomena in everyday talk. They pass without notice; conversational participants do not consider them aberrant, though they do not easily fit into the conventional bounds of the clause (hence the recourse to terminology such as "dislocation," an issue we return to later in the section "Metalanguage").

Likewise, after conventional clause elements have been exhausted, further linguistic matter may arise on the record, as in Examples 29 and 30.

Examples 29 and 30

29. And *he's* quite a comic *the fellow,* you know.

30. [Talking about someone who has just had the disease, shingles] *It* can leave you feeling very weak, it can, though, apparently, *shingles,* can't it.

Here, noun phrase content is left until the end, as it were. Why should this be so? Corpus evidence suggests that these right-dislocated elements have a strong evaluative function, and usually occur in contexts in which speakers are expressing judgements, opinions, stance, and so forth. (Aijmer, 1989; McCarthy & Carter, 1997). It would be wrong, therefore, to dismiss such patterns as "performance phenomena," or "afterthoughts" (see Fretheim, 1995, for a good discussion).

Our criterion here for a spoken grammar must therefore be that elements that occur in unusual word orders as compared to written texts, and elements that do not fit easily into the conventional clause structure, should not be relegated to a dusty corner of the grammar, but should be accorded proper attention, because they play key textual and interpersonal roles in conversation. That such features are not peculiar to English[3] (on right-dislocation see Ashby, 1988, 1994, on French; Heilenman & McDonald, 1993, on French; Fretheim, 1995, on Norwegian) and may well be universal should not tempt us to assume they will simply be automatically assimilated or transferred, and learners may need to be made explicitly aware that such patterns are licensed and perfectly normal in the target language. Exposure to written data alone or absence of reference to such features in pedagogical grammars can only reinforce the prejudice that they are aberrations or irregularities of some sort.

Clause complexes

In the first of our 10 criteria, we raised the problem of units of description, and mentioned the issue of subordination. It is often difficult to assign to a clause the label "subordinate." This is particularly so with what are conventionally termed nonrestrictive *which* clauses. Tao and McCarthy (1998), in a study of a corpus of British and American spoken texts, found that the majority of such clauses were evaluative in function, as typified by Example 31.

Example 31

I can't angle it to shine on the music stand, and the bulb's gone, *which doesn't help.*

They also found that many such clauses occurred after a pause, or after feedback from a listener.

Example 32

Speaker 1: Well actually one person has applied.
Speaker 2: Mm.
Speaker 1: *Which is great.*

---

3 We are often questioned as to whether right-dislocations are a peculiarity of British English, but they certainly occur in U.S. English, as an example from National Public Radio's *Morning Edition* demonstrates: *It's the mattress money of choice, the greenback is.* (On how Russian people hoard U.S. dollars: 8.25.98)

In both cases, the *which* clause seems more like a second main clause (indeed, *which* could be substituted by *and that* in both cases, with no loss of meaning, to produce unequivocal "main" clauses). Speakers seem sometimes to recognize this fact, and main-subordinate "blends" occur.

Example 33

Speaker 1: Nearly a hundred quid a week. But that's the average there, you know.

Speaker 2: Mm.

Speaker 1: *Which it's all relative I suppose.*

In the spoken language, clause complexes need reassessment in terms of what is to be considered main and what subordinate. This principle applies not only to *which* clauses but most notably also to clauses introduced by *because/ 'cos*, where the same indeterminacy applies (for a good discussion of these issues of subordination, see Schleppegrell, 1992).

Other types of clause complexes are rare in everyday conversation, even though they might be quite evident in written texts. This applies to several types of combinations of main and nonfinite subordinate clauses, such as those in Examples 34 and 35.

Examples 34 and 35

34. Both airports were clearly identified as to country, *it* be*ing* explicitly stated that Airport X lacked both radio and tower. (Cambridge International Corpus)

35. First *staged* at the Glasgow Citizens in 1994, and *described* by Williams as being a "comedy of death," the play sees Everett cast brilliantly against type as the rich dying widow Flora Goforth. (*The Observer*, November 26, 1992, p.3)

Once again, corpus evidence strongly argues for a reexamination of the types of clause complexes found in spoken and written language and the need for rethinking the accepted descriptions of main and subordinate clauses.

Unpleasing anomalies

The title of this section refers to the fact that, in examining everyday spoken data, the researcher often encounters features that go against the grain, either of the researcher's own notions of acceptability or of more general feelings among educated users of the language. Occasionally, aberrations do occur in spoken performance (as they do in writing), but there is a difference between

on-off oddities and recurrent, patterned usage distributed across a wide range
of speakers and contexts in a corpus designed to reflect a broad demographic
and social spectrum, as the CANCODE corpus is. When such patterns become
so recurrent that they cannot just be ignored, one has to assimilate them into
the grammar. We have already mentioned *which* clause blends that challenge
the usual rule of nonreduplication of the subject (Example 33); these are by
no means rare, and pass unnoticed in conversation. Example 36 is a further
example.

Example 36

X's has had to be delayed because his teeth were slow
coming, er, coming down, er, *which* fair enough, *that* was
just one of those things, it was unavoidable.

Even more widespread are utterances that seem to contain "double
negatives," but which are natural and common in the speech of all social and
regional groups.

Example 37 and 38

37. It should fit there, cos it's *not* that big I *don't* think.
38. **Speaker 1:** We probably won't see much wildlife.
    Speaker 2: *Not* without binoculars we *won't*.

Both Examples 37 and 38 occur in comment clauses, and this may
be significant in opening the option of apparent double negativity. It is such
potential correlations that spoken grammarians have to take into account when
attempting to explain grammatical choices that defy traditional written norms,
rather than dismissing the spoken examples as aberrant.

Another kind of apparent anomaly that recurs on the corpus across a
wide range of speakers is conditional clause complexes that challenge the rule
that excludes a modal verb from the conditional clause.

Example 39

If *I'd have* stopped I probably would have wondered what
she was going to say. (Instead of *if I had stopped . . .*)

The important criterion here for a spoken grammar is that "irregularities" and anomalies that may go against the grammarian's instincts concerning
correctness or acceptability should first be checked as to their distribution across
speakers and contexts. When a sufficient number of examples from different
speakers in different contexts suggest that a feature is normal and widespread,

then it should be entered in the grammar, even though it may still be deemed unacceptable in more formal contexts or in writing.

Larger sequences

In a recent study, McCarthy (1998, chap. 5) looked at grammatical patterns spanning several sentences or whole paragraphs in written texts and several clauses and/or speaker turns in spoken texts. Based on earlier research, such as that of Zydattiss (1986) and Celce-Murcia (1991), McCarthy's work looked at how sequential patterns of verb tense and aspect varied between spoken and written texts. In some cases, the patterns were the same in both modes, as with the *used to*-plus-*would* sequence, where, in both written and spoken texts, initial *used to* provides a contextual frame for the interpretation of subsequent uses of *would* as "past habitual."

Example 40

Speakers 1 and 2 are describing how they took part in a consumer survey that involved a remote computer automatically ringing their home telephone to collect data in the middle of the night.

Speaker 1: They *used to* you know ring up early hours of the morning, well you *would*, the phone *wouldn't* ring, they*'d* ring that computer.

Speaker 2: And they*'d* read it.

Speaker 3: Yeah.

Speaker 2: And it*'d* go through the phone.

Exactly the same sequence occurs in literary texts, as McCarthy (1998, p. 99) demonstrates. However, a common written (and formal spoken) pattern in news texts, involving initial *be to*-plus-*will*, as in Example 41, is extremely rare in everyday conversation outside of formal contexts such as meetings.

Example 41

ELECTRICITY CHIEFS TO AXE 5,000
Five thousand jobs *are to* be axed by electricity generating firm National Power, it was announced yesterday. Smaller power stations *will* close but bosses pledged no compulsory redundancies over the next five years.

(*Daily Mirror,* July 7, 1990, p. 2)

The same functional sequence of broad reference to determined future events followed by details seems to have as its nearest equivalent in spoken language the sequence *going to*-plus-*will*.

Example 42

Speaker 1 is a health service worker informing Speaker 2 about a new "patient's handbook" that they are producing.

Speaker 1: I'm sort of chairing the working group, em [laughs] a document that, that it's official name *is going to* end up being something like Patient Handbook [Speaker 2: Yeah] but at the moment it, it's lovingly known as the alternative Gideon [Speaker 2:[laughs]] you *'ll* find it on the locker next to the bed or something, yeah.

Observation of extended patterns such as these naturally depend on the willingness of the grammarian to look beyond the bounds of the sentence (or the immediate speaker turn in spoken texts), in other words to take a discourse-grammar perspective (Hughes & McCarthy, 1998). The criterion we wish to press home here is that grammatical patterns exist across longer stretches of text, and that we must take a discoursal perspective that goes beyond the sentence or immediate utterance to establish the degree of overlap or otherwise in such patterns in written and spoken language.

The comparative criterion

This criterion follows directly from the previous section. So far in this chapter we have emphasized difference, that a spoken grammar is in some crucial ways quite a different animal from a written one. The strong form of such a view is misleading, however. Quite clearly, much grammar overlaps between spoken and written, and it would be a disservice to our learners to have them believe that everything has to be learned from square one when the speaking-skills component of the syllabus comes on stream. What is needed is a thorough examination of a spoken corpus side by side with a good, balanced, written one, so that relevant differences can be revealed and entered into the grammar wherever necessary. An example of this might be a comparison of conjunctions as they occur in a spoken corpus and a written one. A pedagogical grammar entry might resemble Fig. 4.1.

Some conjunctions are particularly associated with written or spoken registers and particular positions in those registers. For example, *on the contrary* is very rare in informal conversation. In written English it is more common and usually occurs in front position (or much less frequently in mid-position):

> He had no private understanding with Mr X. On the contrary he knew very little of him.

On the other hand occurs frequently in both spoken and written language. But the concessive adverb *then again* (always in front position) is much more frequent in spoken than written:

> If it had been at the bottom of a councillor's street then I don't think it would ever have been built. But then again that goes on all the time.

Other conjunctions more common in written than spoken language include *accordingly, moreover, furthermore, duly, therefore, as a consequence,* and *in the event.*

Other conjunctions more common in spoken than written language include *what's more, as I say, because of that,* and *in the end.*

Figure 4.1 Linking in written and spoken English.

By the same token, there should be some way of indicating (perhaps as the default condition) areas of the grammar that do not differ from the written usage (e.g., the *used to*-plus-*would* pattern illustrated in a previous section). The comparative criterion is thus a practical one, designed to lessen the load and learning fears for the learner confronting a spoken grammar for the first time. However, a final point needs to be made in relation to written corpora: It is relatively easy to incorporate newspapers and other journalistic texts into a corpus because of ease of availability, access on the Internet, and so forth, but a good written corpus should be as widely sourced as possible to include the kinds of texts people read as a matter of daily routine (not just quality newspapers). This would include mass mailings, tabloid news, magazines, Web pages, E-mails, signs, notices and advertisements, and so forth. Some of these types of written discourse have evolved or are evolving more toward spoken styles, and it may be that the traditional conventions of written grammar, as based on highly literate authors, are not necessarily as highly represented in such text types as we might think. Research with such a balanced corpus might yield a better picture of the cline of usage that exists between formal, literary, and technical texts at one extreme, and casual conversational ones at the other (see Biber, 1988, for an excellent example of such comparative research).

Metalanguage

Throughout this chapter we have struggled, in some places more visibly than others, with a metalanguage that has not always been up to the task of describing the phenomena we would wish to embrace in a spoken grammar. This has been particularly noticeable in the discussions on units and on subordinate and main clauses, where we have often used scare quotes to hide our unease with the terminology. A metalanguage inherited from written-based grammars brings with it its own metaphors and assumptions, which can often create dissonance when applied to spoken data. Nowhere was this more apparent for us than in the section that discusses left- and right-dislocated elements. For one thing, we are unhappy with the notion of "dislocation" or "displacement," because it suggests either that something has been moved or that it is not in its rightful place. We see no evidence in real contexts that anything is in an abnormal position or that real language users have any problems with such forms when they occur. And yet we are at a loss to find a better term to describe the phenomena. In a book in which we offer extracts from the CANCODE corpus for class use, we suggest *heads* (or *topics*) and *tails* as appropriate metaphors for left- and right-dislocation respectively (Carter & McCarthy, 1997, pp. 16, 18), but many may find these terms equally unsatisfactory. What we are in no doubt about is that the metaphors of "left" and "right" are page-driven (and even, for that matter, Western-alphabet page-driven, because other major world writing systems compose their pages vertically or from right-to-left), and totally inappropriate to spoken language, which has no *left* or *right*, only a *now*, a *before*, and a *next*. In this respect, the metaphor of pre- and postposing, as used by Hallidayan grammarians, is slightly less misleading. We do not consider the discussion of metalanguage to be a splitting of hairs: Metaphors are powerful, and the metaphor of the page as the repository of language is an overbearing one in our western cultures. Now that we can investigate language other than on the page (though admittedly, corpus linguists still tend to work with transcripts rather than original audiotapes), we urgently need to evolve a shared metalanguage among the applied linguistic professions that will adequately give form to our understandings of the grammar of everyday talk. Our ninth criterion for a spoken grammar is, therefore, a careful reflection on the metalanguage to be used, and an attempt to devise one that can communicate the special characteristics of the grammar of speech.

Native and nonnative users

Our final criterion relates to the notion of authority in grammatical description. Put simply, the issue is: who is to be the voice of authority with regard to a spoken grammar? The question arises because, in the past, societies have looked to their most highly literate members (usually great writers) in the quest for the establishment of standards of correctness in grammar. No such obvious authorities exist for the grammar of conversation. Equally, we have to take into account that, whereas in writing language users tend to strive towards standard norms within any linguistic community (such that in English, for instance, there are standard written norms embracing the United Kingdom, rather than a northern British, say, or west-country norm), in informal speech variety is of the essence (in the case of Britain there are indeed northern and west-country styles of speaking, along with many others). Variety in this case also includes phonological variation, and this can affect grammatical items as much as lexical ones (e.g., the various British pronunciations of the negative form of *I am*: ai a: nt/, ai elnt/, / ai aemnt/). The evidence of a spoken corpus is only as reliable as the design of the corpus, and thus, as we have already alluded, great care must be taken to ensure that any entry in the spoken grammar is represented in a wide range of speakers of any broad-based linguistic community as defined by the grammarian for practical purposes (e.g., North American English, Mexican Spanish, Swiss German).

However, in the case of widely used languages such as English, Mandarin Chinese, or Spanish a further question arises, and that is: Should the spoken grammar of a language be that of the speakers of the original, colonizing language, or should it be that of its present-day users? This issue is particularly acute in the case of English, which has taken over as lingua franca in numerous domains across the globe, such that it is no longer controversial to speculate that its native speakers are in a minority among the total number of its daily users. There are extreme answers to the question posed, and some less extreme. One extreme answer is to say that one norm is required, and that that norm should emanate from the dominant colonizing community (candidates for which, in different parts of the world, in the case of English, would be British, American, or Australian varieties). This answer is quite understandably offensive to many highly proficient or near-native users of English in communities where robust local varieties have evolved (e.g., Malaysian English). Another extreme answer is to say that a spoken grammar should be as varied as its users. Clearly there are both practical and theoretical problems here; this would require a massive collection of data beyond the resources of most organizations (though the International Corpus of English (ICE) corpus project at present comes the closest to achieving this aim; see Nelson, 1996), and it is theoretically very difficult to delimit the boundaries of varieties (we have suggested how difficult it is simply to delimit a variety called "British spoken English"). Compromise solutions include targeting those nations where a language such as English has official status and is in daily use, but such a solution excludes the millions of business and professional users of English who communicate in our new global village in spoken English. The most realistic solution, at least for the present, would seem to be to have a variety of spoken corpora (some country-based, some more regionally or globally based, some native-speaker, some nonnative, some mixed, etc.), which could be cross-compared to establish a core set of grammatical features in wide international usage.

Shifting the balance away from the native speakers of colonizing communities has important implications for the basic concept and status of the native speaker. Just as a corpus of nonnative speaker speech will contain a wide range of speakers of varying degrees of proficiency, so too will any native-speaker corpus, and it becomes more difficult and complicated to decide who are the most "expert" users of a language like English, since many nonnative users will clearly be more proficient communicators and users of English than many native speakers. We thus alter the focus and enter the territory of *expert users* of a language as those to whom we may look as models, regardless of their status as native or nonnative speakers. We have no easy way at the moment of distinguishing who these users are; we have no spoken equivalent of an international literary canon of English. Nor perhaps should we even consider going down that path if we wish to be truly democratic in our description of English, in which case we are left with the (probably limited) resources of whatever corpora are available to us, and reliance on statistical evidence across groups of users (native and nonnative), without evaluation of their expertise as users, as to what should and should not be included in a more internationally motivated grammar of spoken English.

Our tenth criterion thus leaves us with more questions than answers, but it is no less important for that. The point to be underscored here is that the spoken language raises more immediate questions about the authority of its users than does the written, and where languages have become international lingua francas, the question of variation will almost certainly be uppermost. It is one that corpus linguistics can only partially solve, and one that raises as many ideological questions as linguistic ones.

Conclusion

The need to investigate spoken grammars is, we believe, an urgent one within the language teaching profession. Already committed as most of us are to a communicative methodology that stresses the importance of speaking skills, any well-evidenced information about how people actually use grammar in everyday talk must be a bonus to us. What is more, in world where communications are developing so rapidly, it can only be a matter of years before anyone, anywhere in the world, can speak directly to anyone else in real time, easily and cheaply. In that world, spoken language, and the mastery of lingua franca (whether it be English or whatever replaces it) will be an empowering skill. We have argued that spoken grammar highlights the textual and interpersonal aspects of messages because of its face-to-face nature; it would be a severe injustice if we, as a profession, refused to investigate its grammar, or closed our eyes to what we can know about how real users use it in everyday life in order to help our learners become better global communicators. Our 10 criteria are probably not the only possible ones, and readers are invited to add their 11th or 12th. However, the 10 we have discussed have served the present authors as useful constraints in our own research and our applications of that research in the practical arena (see Carter, Hughes, & McCarthy, 1999). We certainly view the design and implementation of spoken grammars as one of the most challenging areas in the practice of language teaching today.

References

Aijmer, K. (1989). Themes and tails: The discourse function of dislocated elements. *Nordic Journal of Linguistics, 12,* 137–154.

Ashby, W. (1988). The syntax, pragmatics, and sociolinguistics of left- and right-dislocations in French. *Lingua, 75,* 203–229.

Ashby, W. (1994). An acoustic profile of right-dislocations in French. *French Language Studies, 4,* 127–145.

Biber, D. (1988). *Variation across speech and writing.* Cambridge, UK: Cambridge University Press.

Blasco, M. (1995). Dislocation et thématisation en français parlé. *Recherche sur le Français Parlé, 13,* 45–65.

Brown, P., & Levinson, S. (1987). *Politeness: Some universals in language usage.* Cambridge, UK: Cambridge University Press.

Carter, R. A., Hughes, R., & McCarthy, M. J. (1998). Telling tails: Grammar, the spoken language and materials development. In B. Tomlinson (Ed.) *Materials development in language teaching.* (pp. 67–86). Cambridge, UK: Cambridge University Press.

Carter, R. A., Hughes, R., & McCarthy, M. J. (1999). *Exploring English grammar in context.* Cambridge, UK: Cambridge University Press.

Carter, R. A., & McCarthy, M. J. (1995a). Discourse and creativity: Bridging the gap between language and literature. In G. Cook & B. Seidlhofer (Eds.) *Principle and practice in applied linguistics. Studies in honour of H. G. Widdowson* (pp. 303–321). Oxford: Oxford University Press.

Carter, R. A., & McCarthy, M. J. (1995b). Grammar and the spoken language. *Applied Linguistics, 16,* 141–158.

Carter, R. A., & McCarthy, M. J. (1997). *Exploring Spoken English.* Cambridge, UK: Cambridge University Press.

Carter, R. A., & McCarthy, M. J. (1999). The English *get*-passive in spoken discourse: Description and implications for an interpersonal grammar. *English Language and Linguistics, 3,* 41–58.

Celce-Murcia, M. (1991). Discourse analysis and grammar instruction. *Annual Review of Applied Linguistics, 11,* 135–151.

Chappell, H. (1980). Is the *get*-passive adversative? *Papers in Linguistics, 13,* 411-452.

Collins-COBUILD. (1990). *Collins-COBUILD English grammar.* London: HarperCollins.

Eastwood, J. (1994). *Oxford guide to English grammar.* Oxford: Oxford University Press.

Fretheim, T. (1995). Why Norwegian right-dislocated phrases are not afterthoughts. *Nordic Journal of Linguistics, 18,* 31–54.

Geluykens, R. (1989). The syntactization of interactional processes: Some typological evidence. *Belgian Journal of Linguistics, 4,* 91–103.

Geluykens, R. (1992). *From discourse process to grammatical construction: On left-dislocation in English.* Amsterdam: John Benjamins.

Halliday, M. A. K. (1961). Categories of the theory of grammar. *Word, 17,* 241–292.

Halliday, M. A. K. (1991). Corpus studies and probabilistic grammar. In K. Aijmer & B. Altenberg (Eds.), *English corpus linguistics* (pp. 30–43). London: Longman.

Halliday, M. A. K. (1992). Language as system and language as instance: The corpus as a theoretical construct. In J. Svartvik (Ed.), *Directions in corpus linguistics* (pp. 61–77). Berlin: Mouton de Gruyter.

Heilenman, L. K., & McDonald, J. L. (1993). Dislocated sequences and word order in French: A processing approach. *Journal of French Language Studies, 3,* 165–190.

Hockett, C. (1986). Grammar for the hearer. In G. McGregor (Ed.), *Language for hearers* (pp. 49–68). Oxford: Pergamon.

Hughes, R. & McCarthy, M. J. (1998). From sentence to discourse: Discourse grammar and English language teaching. *TESOL Quarterly, 32,* 263–287.

Itkonen, E. (1980). Qualitative vs quantitative analysis in linguistics. In T. Perry (Ed.), *Evidence and argumentation in linguistics* (pp. 334–366). Berlin: Mouton de Gruyter.

Lerner, G. H. (1991). On the syntax of sentences-in-progress. *Language in Society, 20,* 441–458.

McCarthy, M. J. (1995). Conversation and literature: tense and aspect. In J. Payne (Ed.), *Linguistic approaches to literature* (pp. 58–73). Birmingham: University of Birmingham, English Language Research.

McCarthy, M. J. (1998). *Spoken language and applied linguistics.* Cambridge, UK: Cambridge University Press.

McCarthy, M. J., & Carter, R. A. (1995). What is spoken grammar and how should we teach it? *ELT Journal, 49,* 207–218.

McCarthy, M. J., & Carter, R. A. (1997). Grammar, tails and affect: Constructing expressive choices in discourse. *Text, 17,* 405–429.

Nelson, G. (1996). The design of the corpus. In S. Greenbaum (Ed.), *Comparing English worldwide: The International Corpus of English* (pp. 27–35). Oxford: Oxford University Press.

Nesbitt, C., & Plum, G. (1988). Probabilities in a systemic-functional grammar: The clause complex in English. In R. Fawcett & D. Young (Eds.), *New developments in systemic linguistics: Vol. 2, Theory and applications* (pp. 6–38). London: Pinter.

Palmer, H. E., & Blandford, F. G. (1969). *A Grammar of spoken English* (3rd ed.). Cambridge, UK: Heffer..

Paprotté, W. (1988). A discourse perspective on tense and aspect in standard modern Greek and English. In B. Rudzka-Ostyn (Ed.), *Topics in cognitive linguistics* (pp. 447–505). Amsterdam: John Benjamins.

Rivero, M. (1980). On left-dislocation and topicalization in Spanish. *Linguistic Inquiry, 11,* 363–393.

Schiffrin, D. (1981). Tense variation in narrative. *Language, 57,* 45–62.

Schleppegrell, M. (1992). Subordination and linguistic complexity. *Discourse Processes, 15,* 117–131.

Silva-Coryalán, C. (1983). Tense and aspect in oral Spanish narrative: Context and meaning. *Language, 59,* 760–780.

Soga, M. (1983). *Tense and aspect in modern colloquial Japanese.* University of British Columbia Press.

Svartvik, J. (1966). *On voice in the English verb.* The Hague: Mouton.

Swan, M. (1995). *Practical English Usage.* Oxford: Oxford University Press.

Tao, H., & McCarthy, M. J. (1999, July). *Redefining non-restrictive which-clauses, which is not an easy thing.* Paper presented at the Speech and Writing Conference, University of Nottingham, 1999.

Waugh, L. (1991). Tense-aspect and hierarchy of meanings: pragmatic, textual, modal, discourse, expressive, referential. In L. Waugh & S. Rudy (Eds.), *New vistas in grammar: Invariance and variation* (pp. 241–259). Amsterdam: John Benjamins.

Wolfson, N. (1978). A feature of performed narrative: The conversational historical present. *Language in Society, 7,* 215–237.

Wolfson, N. (1979). The conversational historical present alternation. *Language, 55,* 168–182.

Zydatiss, W. (1986). Grammatical categories and their text functions – some implications for the content of reference grammars. In G. Leitner (Ed.), *The English reference grammar: Language and linguistics, writers and readers* (pp. 140–155). Tübingen: Max Niemeyer Verlag.